Every child should have the chance to dream. Pete Castle | Father

b   a

a celebration in words & photographs

b y

David Ellwand

Candlewick Press

Cambridge, Massachusetts

It sometimes happens, even in the best of families, that a baby is born.

This is not necessarily cause for alarm. The important thing is to keep

your wits about you and borrow some money.   Elinor Goulding Smith | Author

u n i q u e

What makes my child different and special?

On a bad night, only his fingerprints!

Lisa Davies | Mother

This book is full of babies, but you won't hear their crying and you won't have to

change their diapers. On the other hand, you will be able to imagine what it's like

to touch their petal-soft skin, feel their tiny fingers curl around yours, and receive

 their sweet smiles. Their parents will really have these experiences,

and more, but unless they're very lucky, it will all go by in a blur.

[an introduction]

Before long, their "babies" will be borrowing the keys to the family car and heading

f i r s t

off on their grown-up paths. This book is an attempt to capture the fleeting

moments of babyhood, when each unique personality is emerging to find its place

in the world. These babies do not know what lies ahead in their lives, but nature

propels them forward to new experiences. We wish them all the best with the adventure.

It was the tiniest thing
I ever decided to put my whole *life* into.

Terri Guillemets | Author

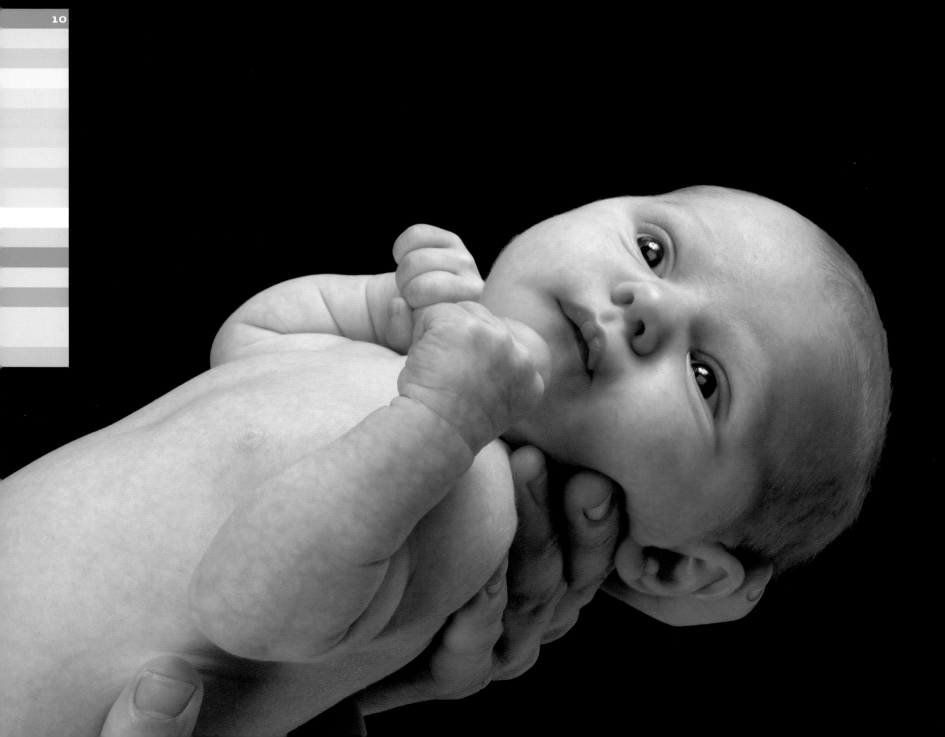

lily | purity

[welcome to the world]

h e l l o

pitter, patter . . .

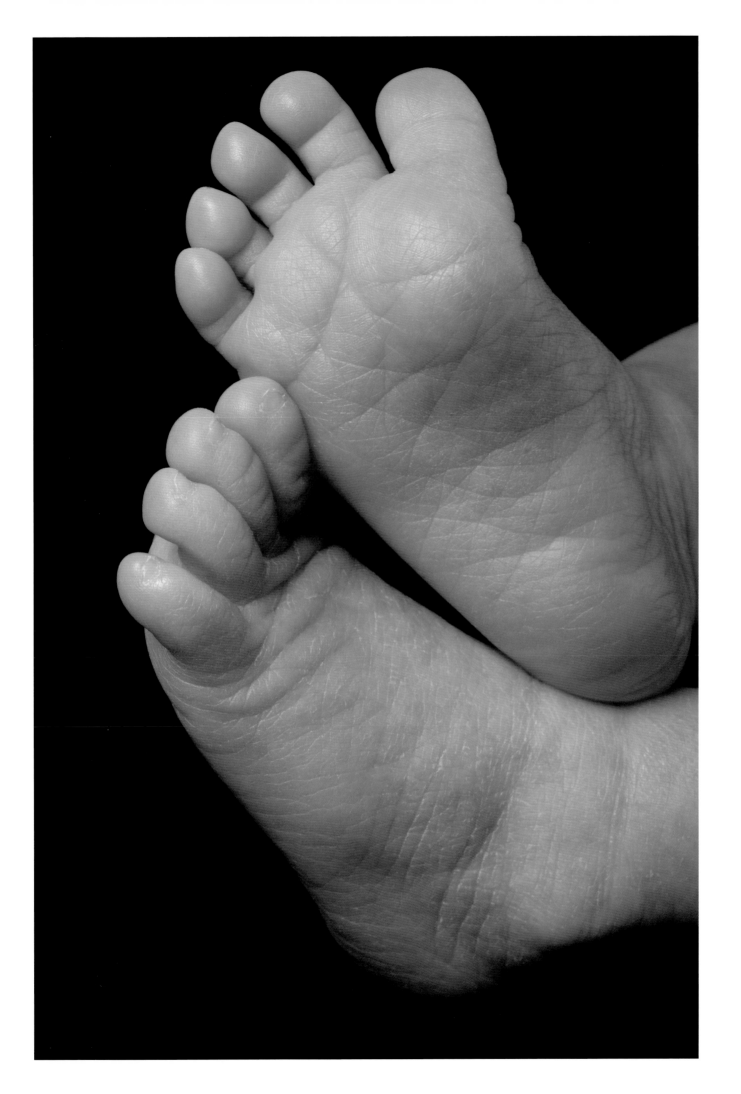

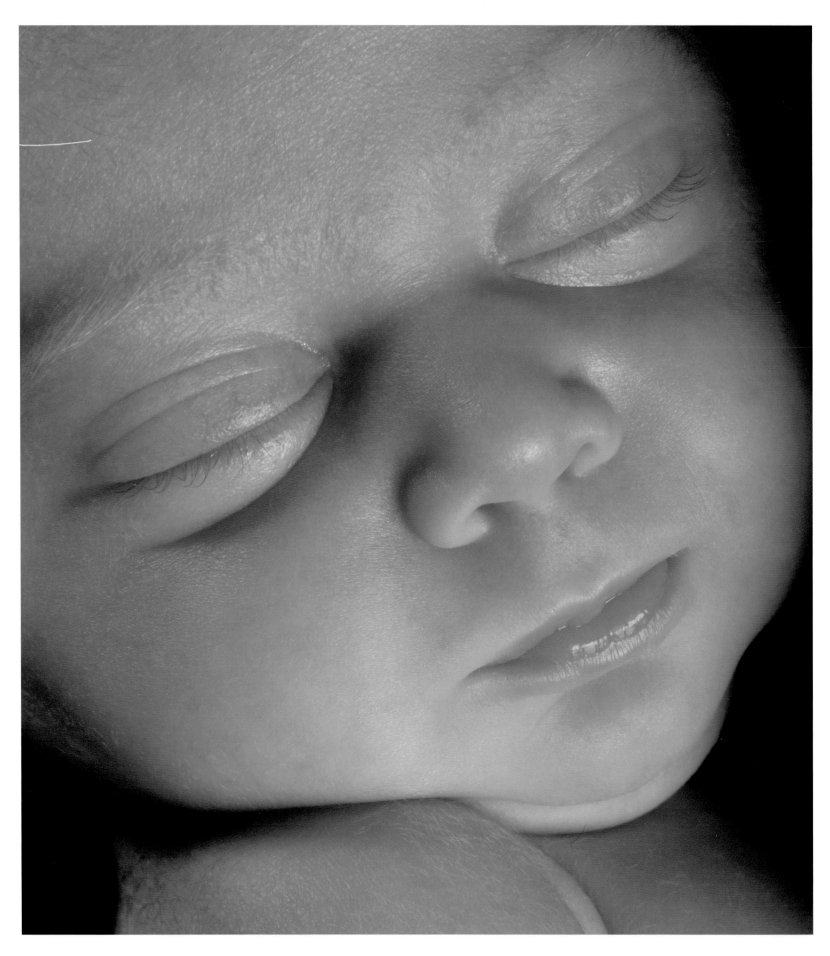

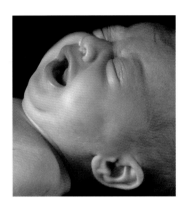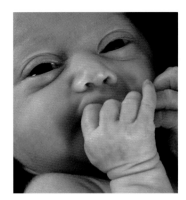

Babies are necessary to grown-ups. A new baby is like the beginning

When you were born, you cried

of all things — wonder, hope, a dream of possibilities. . . . Babies are

and the world rejoiced.

almost the only remaining link with nature, with the natural world of

Native American proverb

living things from which we spring.

Eda Le Shan | Educator & author

In
the
sheltered
simplicity
of the
first few
days after
a baby is born,
one sees again the
magical
closed circle,
the miraculous
sense of two people
existing only for each other.

Anne Morrow Lindbergh | Aviator & author

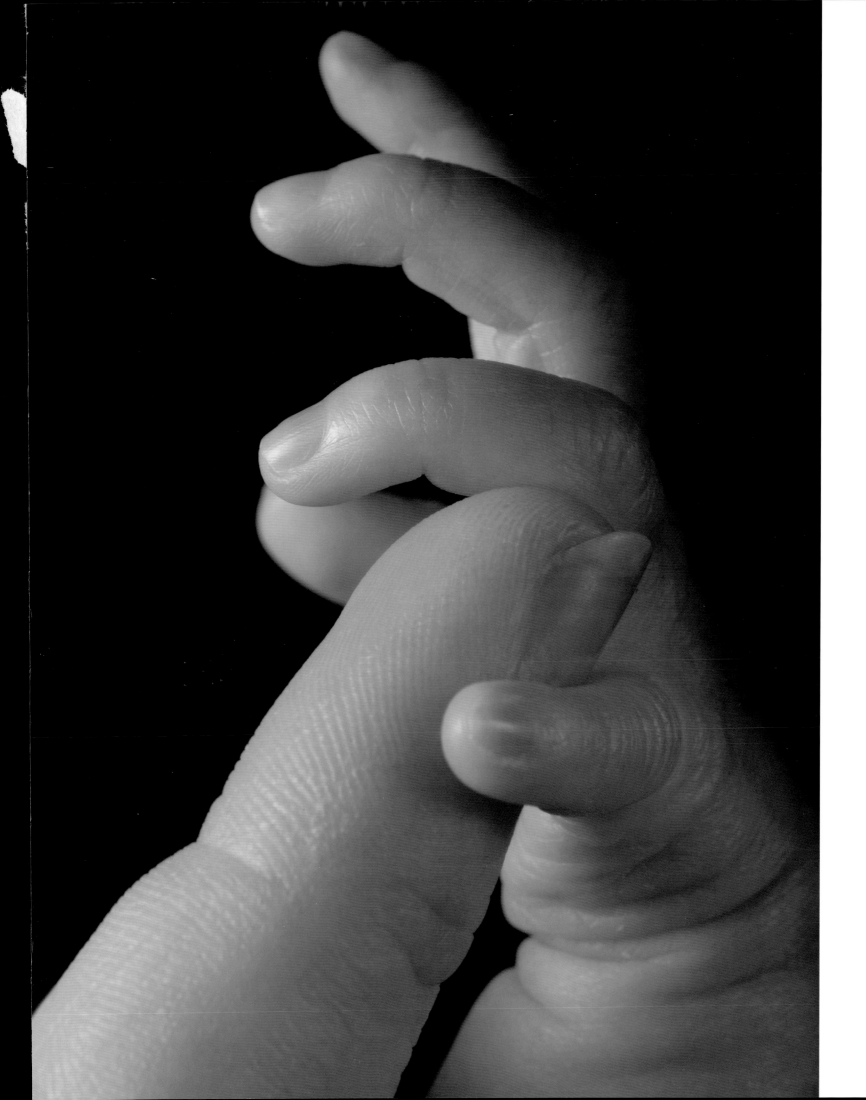

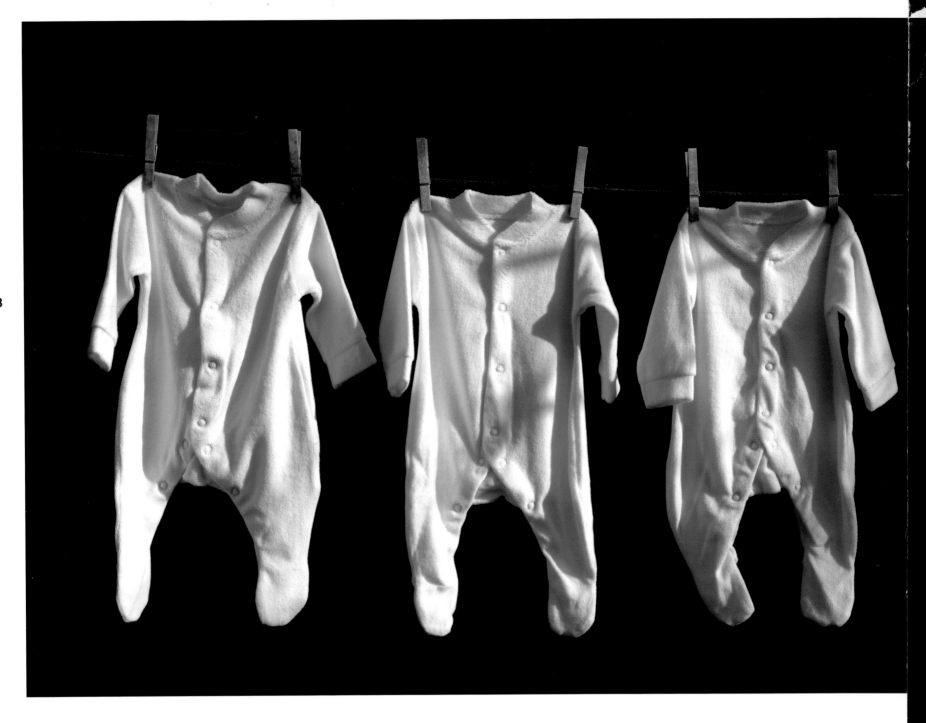

Even when freshly washed and relieved of all obvious

18 billion diapers are used in the U.S. every year. If laid end to end, they would reach to the moon.

confections, children tend to be sticky.   Fran Lebowitz | Author & humorist

Laundry takes on a whole new meaning! It's like washing for an army of little soldiers.   Sue Harry | New mother

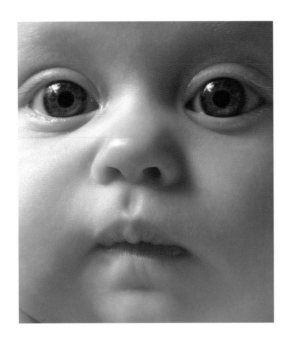 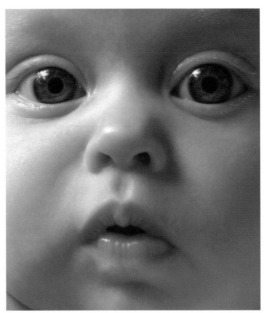 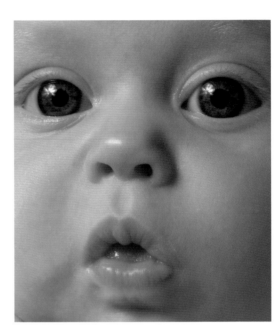

At 9 weeks . . .

I think I see something deeper, more infinite, more *eternal* than the ocean in the expression of the eyes of a little baby. Vincent Van Gogh | Artist

. . . at 9 months

[unconditional and forever]

love

A rose with all its sweetest leaves yet folded.

Lord Byron | Poet

24 How impossible it seems that one day the knitted booties will

be replaced by soccer cleats, the innocent gurgles will give way to

solemn vows. Rose Jarman | Mother

A baby is an *angel* whose wings decrease as his legs increase.

French proverb

Life is not a matter of milestones, but of moments.

Rose Fitzgerald Kennedy | Mother

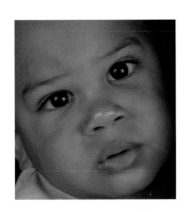

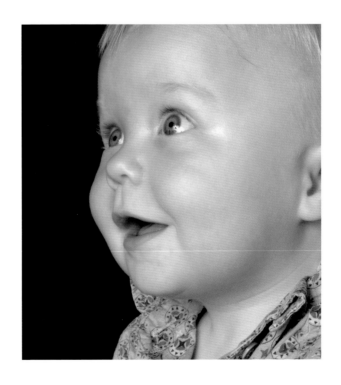

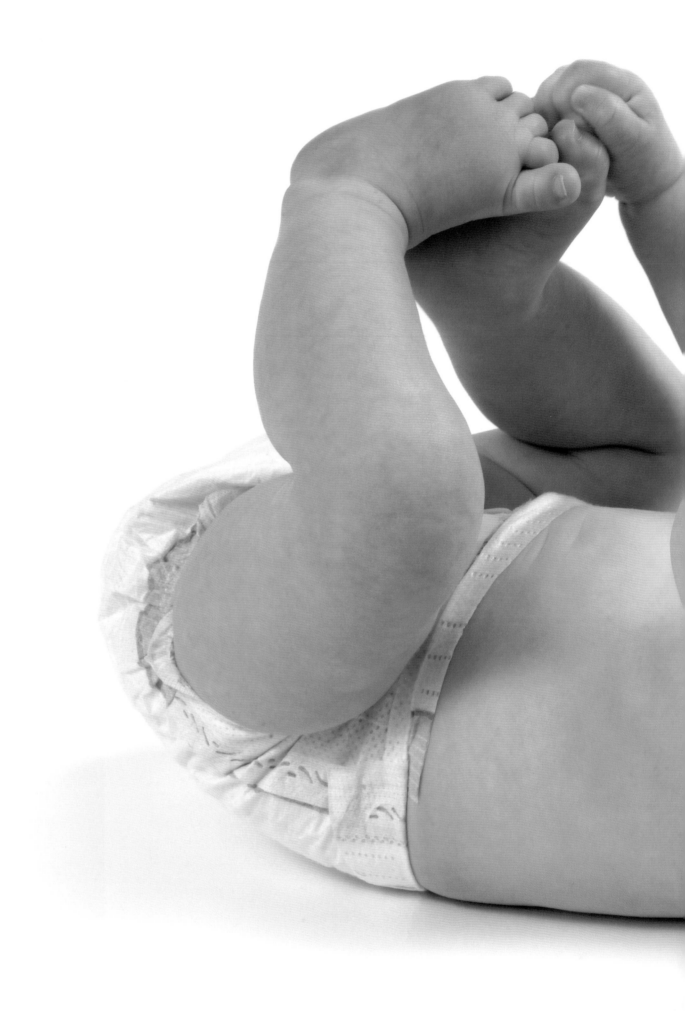

It is the nature of babies to be in bliss.   Deepak Chopra | Author   **29**

Allow children to be happy in their OWN way; for what better way will they ever find?

Dr. Samuel Johnson | Scholar & author

Before you were conceived, I wanted you.
Before you were born, I loved you.
Before you were here an hour, I would die for you.
                                        This is the miracle of Love.

Maureen Hawkins | Poet

A baby will make love stronger, days shorter, nights longer, bankroll smaller, home happier, clothes shabbier, the past forgotten, and the future worth living for.   Anonymous

Loving a baby or child is a circular business, a kind of feedback loop. The more you give the more you get

and the more you get the more you feel like giving...

Penelope Leach | Child psychologist & author

emotion

[quick to laugh . . . quick to cry]

crocus | cheerfulness

If your baby is beautiful and perfect, never cries and fusses, sleeps on schedule

Be gentle with the young.   Juvenal | Roman satirist

and burps on demand, an angel all the time, you're the grandma.

Teresa Bloomingdale | Author

Little girls are the nicest things that happen to people.

They are born with a little bit of angelshine in them

and though it wears thin sometimes

there is always enough to lasso your heart.

Alan Beck | Author

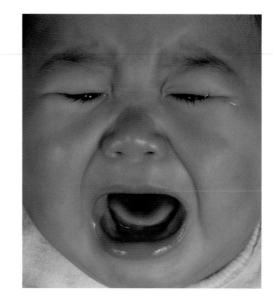

Adam and Eve had many advantages,

but the principal one was that they escaped teething.

Mark Twain | Author

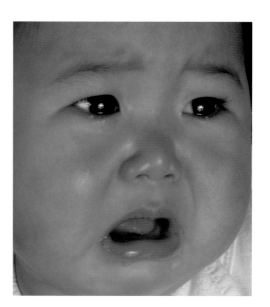

The crying gives way to hiccupy *sighs*,
and tears dry on your cheek as their breathing
quiets and sleep arrives. What relief!

Suzannah Mitchell | Mother

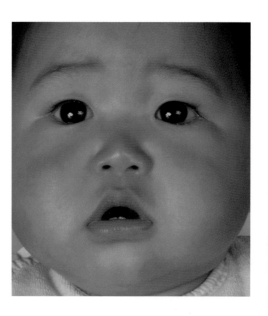

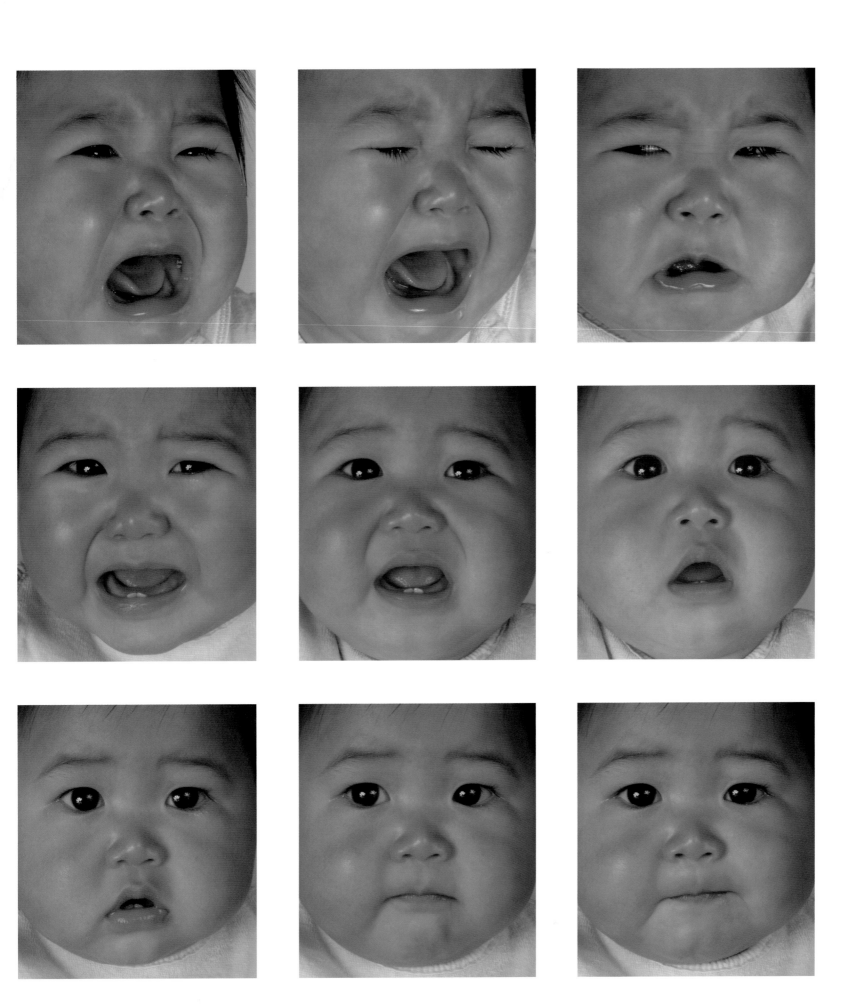

A boy is a magical creature — you can lock him
out of your workshop, but you can't lock him
out of your heart. You can get him out of your
study, but you can't get him out of your mind.

Alan Beck | Author

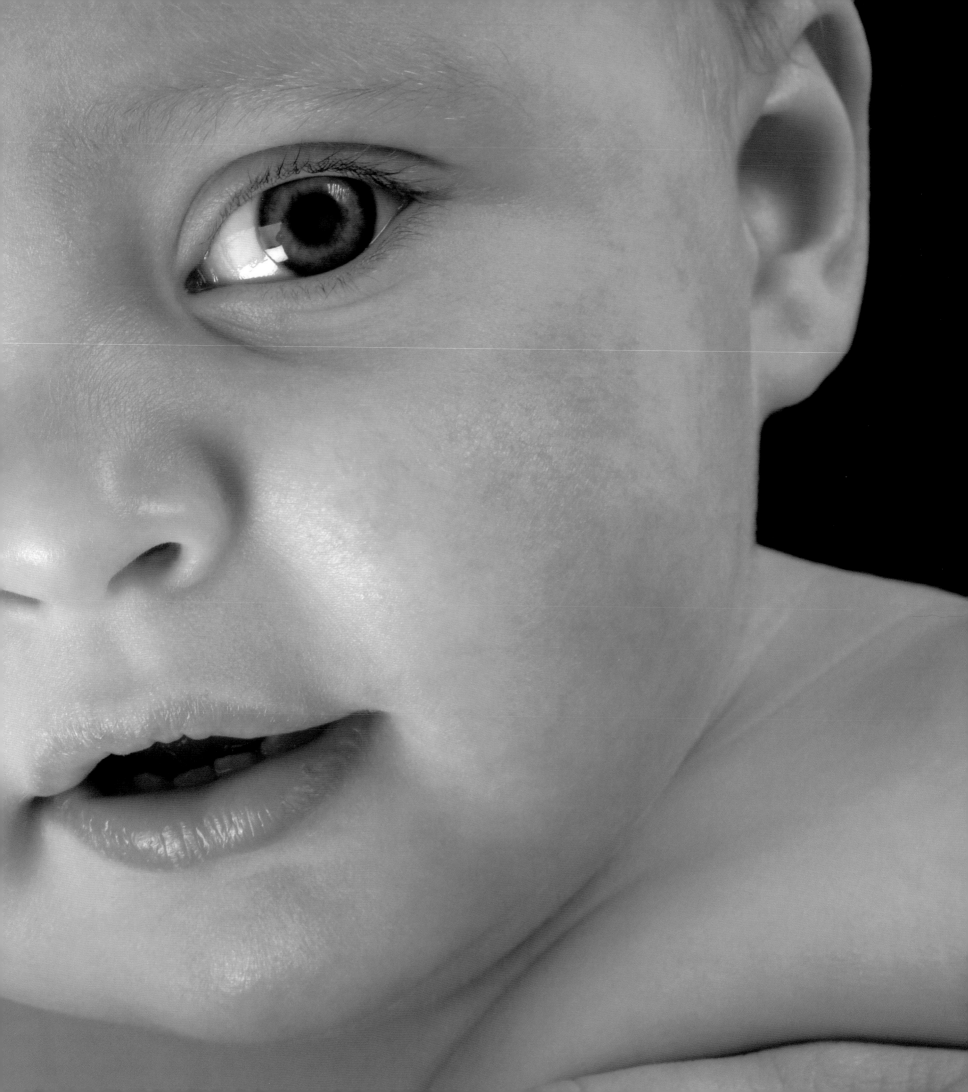

If you can give your son or daughter only one gift, let it be enthusiasm.

Bruce Barton | Author & advertising executive

There are two lasting bequests
we can hope to give our children.
One of these is roots,
the other, **Wings**.

Hodding Carter | Journalist & author

s e l f

[this is me]

I am not a glutton — I am an explorer of food.

Erma Bombeck | Author & humorist

Play is often talked about as if it was

But for children play is

Play is the real work

a relief from serious learning.

serious learning.

of childhood.

Fred Rogers | Children's television personality

54

Many things can wait; the child cannot.
Now is the time his bones are being formed,
his mind is being developed.
To him, we cannot say tomorrow,
his name is today. Gabriela Mistral | Poet

I do not love him because he is good, but because he is my little child.   Rabindranath Tagore | Author   **55**

If you think it's hard in the beginning, wait till they're mobile. . . .

Margaret Bird | Mother

The one thing that children wear out

faster than shoes is parents.

John J. Plomp | Zoologist

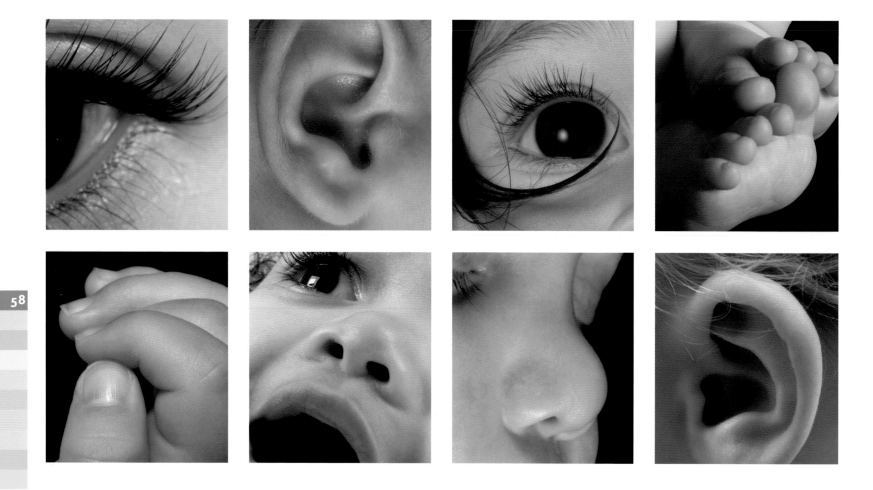

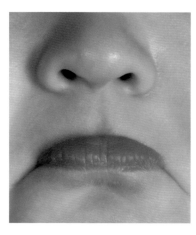
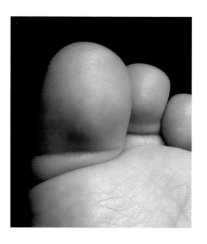
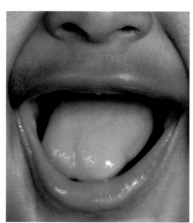

58

Children, like animals, use all their senses
to discover the world.

Eudora Welty | Author

u   n

64 There are two things in this life for which we are never prepared

and that is twins. Josh Billings | Humorist

Double the trouble . . . double the joy!

Tom Moore | Father of twins

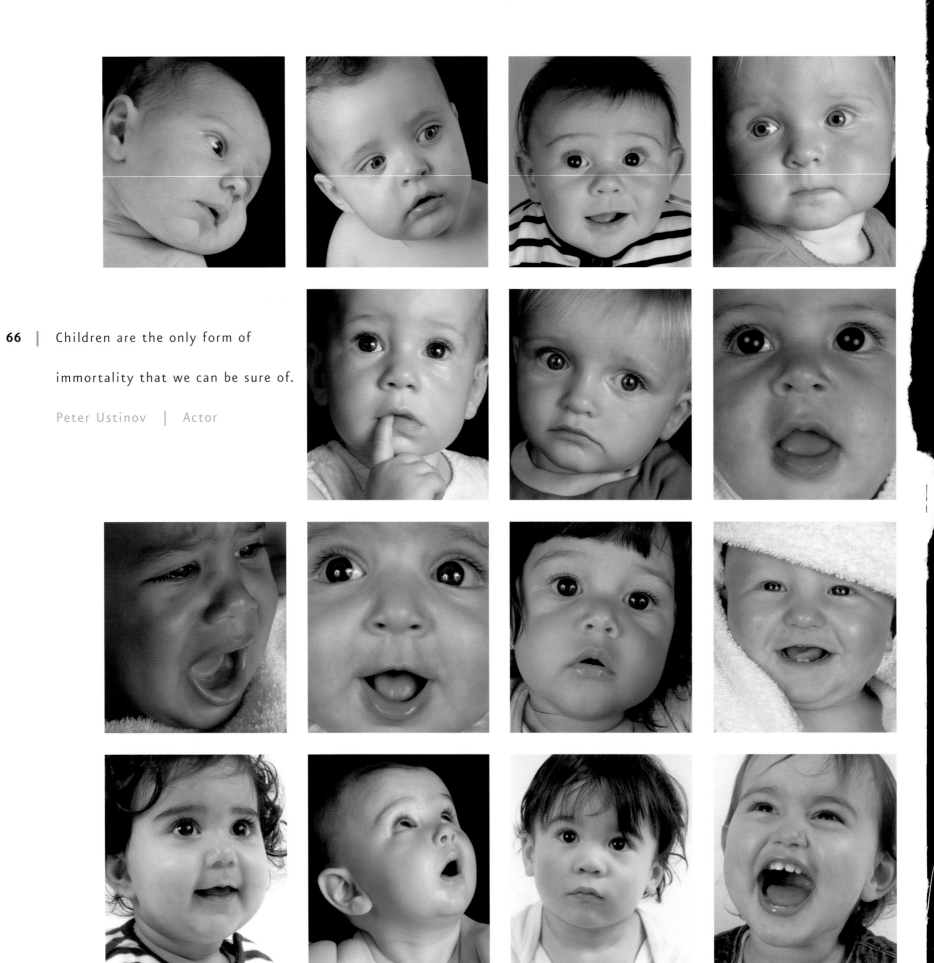

66 | Children are the only form of

immortality that we can be sure of.

Peter Ustinov | Actor

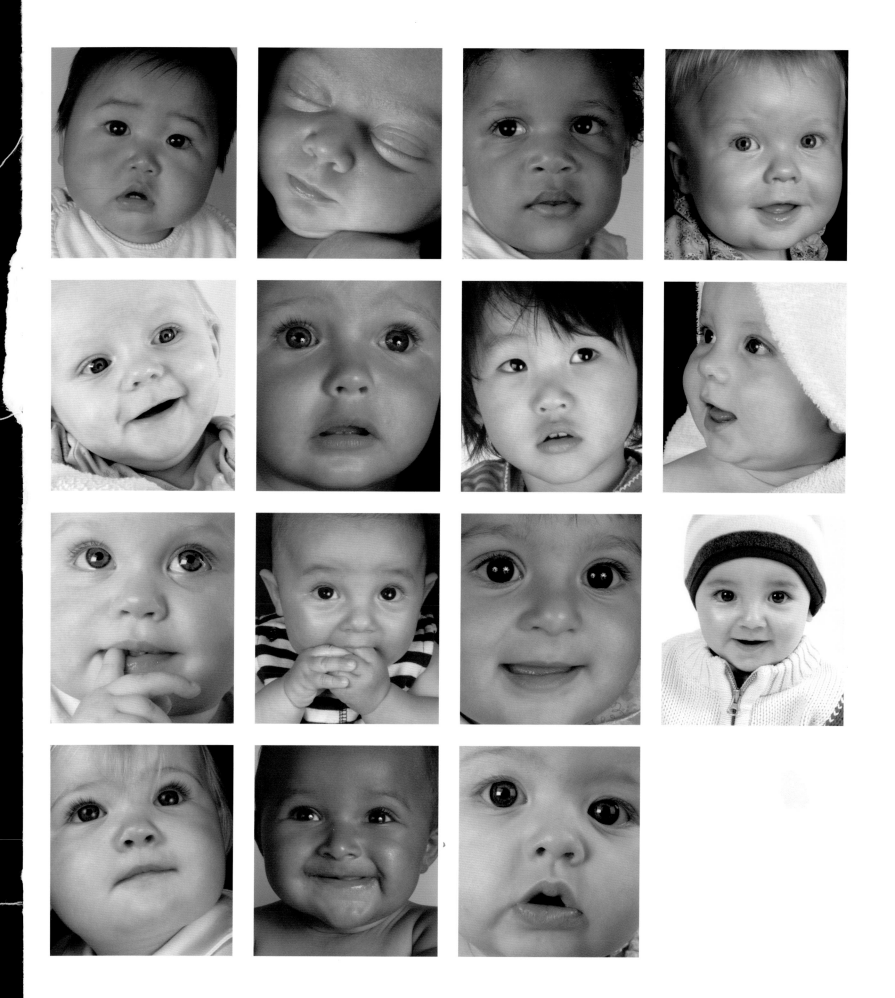

Our children are not going to be just "our children"—they are

going to be other people's husbands and wives and the parents

of our grandchildren. Mary S. Calderone | Physician & author

Your children will always be your babies,

even if they have gray hair.

Janet Leigh | Actress

p. 10 From www.quotegarden.com, copyright © 1998–2004 by Terri Guillemets

p. 16 From GIFT FROM THE SEA by Anne Morrow Lindbergh, copyright © 1955, 1975, renewed 1983 by Anne Morrow Lindbergh. Used by permission of Pantheon Books, a division of Random House, Inc.

p. 29 From the book The Seven Laws of Spiritual Success © 1994, Deepak Chopra. Reprinted by permission of Amber-Allen Publishing, Inc. P.O. Box 6657, San Rafael, CA 94903. All rights reserved.

p. 35 Your Baby and Child, Penelope Leach 1977, London, p.10 Copyright © Dorling Kindersley Limited, London, 1977, 1988, 1997, 2003 Text copyright © Penelope Leach, 1977, 1988, 1997, 2003. Reproduced by permission of Dorling Kindersley Ltd.

p. 58 Reprinted by permission of the publisher from ONE WRITER'S BEGINNINGS by Eudora Welty, p.10, Cambridge, Mass.: Harvard University Press, Copyright © 1983, 1984 by Eudora Welty.

p. 62 "The world tips away when we look into our children's faces." (pp. 4) from THE BLUE JAY'S DANCE by LOUISE ERDRICH Copyright © 1995 by Louise Erdrich. Reprinted by permission of HarperCollins Publishers Inc.

First edition 2004

Library of Congress Cataloging-in-Publication Data is available.

Library of Congress Catalog Card Number 2004045857.

ISBN 0-7636-2606-6

1 2 3 4 5 6 7 8 9 10

Printed in Belgium

This book was typeset in Eureka Sans & Braganza. The photographs were taken using a Fuji S2 digital camera fitted with a 60mm micro Nikkor lens, lit by Elinchrom flash, then processed using Apple computers running Adobe software.

Photographer's assistant: Rebecca Fairbairn
Models & styling by Caroline Repchuk
Designed by Mike Jolley and edited by Sue Harris, The Templar Company plc

First published in the United States and Canada by Candlewick Press
2067 Massachusetts Avenue
Cambridge, Massachusetts 02140

visit us at www.candlewick.com

David Ellwand would like to thank Alfie, Amber, Arthur, Asha, Ayana, Bayley,

Caroline, Charlie, Crystal, Daniel, Daisey, Ellie, Ellesia, Emily, Esta, Fletcher,

Florence, Freya, Isaac, Jade, Jamie C., Jamie K., Jude, Lilli-Rose, Lleyton,

Matthew, Molly, Nathan, Noah, Queenie, Reuben, Rosie, Rosie-Beth, Sam,

Tegan, Thorne, and last but by no means least, Zoe, for their

unique roles in this book.

l a s t

[but not least]